Library of Congress Control Number: 2025908242

ISBN: 979-8-9986488-0-9

Hugo Finds a Home

Book 1 in the Hugo's Hijinks Series

Written & Illustrated by:
Heather Denton

Dedication:

Thank you to Hugo's foster moms who poured their love and time into him.

Thank you to my husband, Craig, for listening to my ramblings about what I had to do next for this book, for posing for illustrations and for supporting my dream of getting Hugo's story out to the world.

There was this zoomie little pup who, like other puppies, was full of energy - running here and there with all of his littermates.

One cozy afternoon, the puppies' mom told them all about forever homes. She told them they were filled with love, cuddles, and new best friends. She told them they would go to their forever homes soon.

Before he knew it, the puppy was on his way to a new family.

When he arrived at his new home he was very frightened.
It was loud and the kids tugged on his ears and pulled his tail.

The big people
wouldn't
listen
to him when
he tried
to tell them
that he
had to go potty.

They would get mad and scold him
for having accidents.

He didn't understand
why they
would get mad.

They never taught him
what
"sit" or "stay" meant.

Then, one day, the puppy
was sent to live
with another family.

And another...

His fear grew with
each new family.

and another...

and still another!

When the puppy was a year old, he was sent to live
in a foster home - a warm, caring place where he would stay until his
forever home was found.

His foster moms loved him . . .

trained him. . .

I hope I'm doing this right.

and took him for walks.

Time went by . . .

and the puppy
wondered if he
would ever find his
forever home.

Then, one day, his foster moms told him that two people were coming to meet him. He wondered if this was the day he had been waiting for.

When he met the two people
they had treats for him, played ball with him,
and he even rolled over so they
could rub his belly.

But then they left and
he didn't understand why.

The very next day, his foster moms were putting all of
his things in the car. Before he knew it, they
were on the road-and he still didn't know what was happening.

They drove for a little while, but when they stopped, he saw the people come out of the house- and he was so happy!
He couldn't stop wagging his tail.
It was the people he had met yesterday!
He could hardly believe it. He hoped they had treats.

He was home! He went straight into the house and laid on the couch.

The people laughed joyfully. They said they were his mom and dad and they told him his name is "Hugo."

Discussion:

If you could adopt a dog, what color would it be?

What would you teach your dog?

What would you name your dog?

What kind of places would you take your dog?

If you see someone walking a dog, what should you do before petting the dog?

Author's Note

My husband and I have 3 dogs and a cat. Hugo is very special to both of us, but I feel like Hugo and I have a special bond. Hugo is a mix of American Pitbull Terrier, Staffordshire Terrier, and Border Collie. He is so much fun to be around. He still has fears due to his past, but we are so grateful to have such a special dog in our life. Hugo loves to go camping, going on road trips, and walking or hiking. He especially loves staying in hotels (mostly sleeping on hotel beds), and his all time favorite pass time is sleeping. My hope for this series is that the reader will see a new side to the American Pitbull Terrier. The real side of this amazing family dog.

First picture we saw of Hugo.

Craig cuddling Hugo.

Heather petting Hugo when he first came home.

Craig's first meeting with Hugo. (Heather was there but not pictured).

Book 2 preview

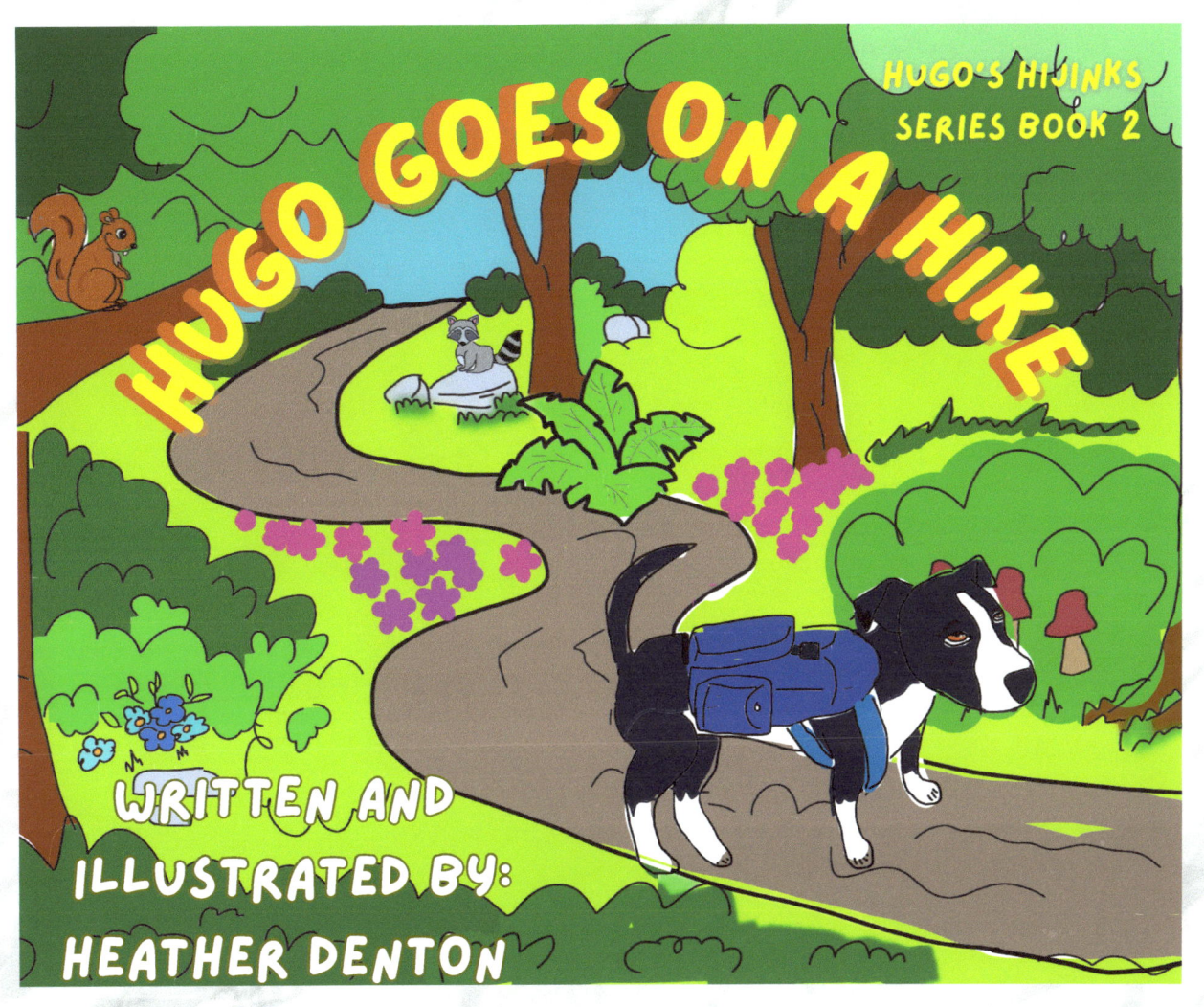

www.ingramcontent.com/pod-product-compliance
Lightning Source LLC
Chambersburg PA
CBHW040819120626

46551CB00004B/601